The
Xenophobe's®
guide to the
BELGIANS

Antony Mason

Oval Books

Published by Oval Books
5 St. John's Buildings
Canterbury Crescent
London SW9 7QH
United Kingdom

Telephone: +44 (0)20 7733 8585
E-mail: info@ovalbooks.com
Web site: www.ovalbooks.com

First published by Ravette Publishing, 1995
Reprinted 1997, 1998

First published by Oval Books, 1999
Updated 2000, 2001, 2004, 2005, 2007

Editor – Catriona Tulloch Scott
Series Editor – Anne Tauté

Cover design – Jim Wire, Quantum
Printer – J.H. Haynes & Co Ltd
Producer – Oval Projects Ltd

Xenophobe's® is a Registered Trademark.

ISBN-13: 978-1-902825-19-9
ISBN-10: 1-902825-19-5

Contents

The Belgian population is 10 million compared with 5 million Danes, 7 million Swiss, 16 million Dutch, 45 million Spanish, 50 million English, 60 million French, 59 million Italians and 82 million Germans.

The population is divided into two main language groups with about 6 million Dutch speakers and 4 million French speakers (plus 67,000 German speakers living on the German border). Brussels upsets this neat division by being a primarily French-speaking pocket within Flemish territory.

Belgium is about a quarter of the size of England, and could fit into France 18 times.

Nationalism and Identity

Belgians are not publicly fervent about their nationality. In a recent opinion poll it was found that 60% of Belgians wish they had been born elsewhere. Their national anthem goes on about *la Patrie* (which is made to rhyme with '*O Belgique! O Mère chérie*', poor thing), but few Belgians can get beyond the first verse. One prospective Belgian prime minister, when asked if he knew the words, began singing the *Marseillaise*.

The fact that Brussels is the capital of Belgium is a good thing for the Belgians, because the city's status as 'the capital of Europe' means that people all over the world have at last been able to place their country (roughly) on the map. This won't necessarily mean that foreigners will know what language the Belgians speak, but it's a start.

Forewarned

For want of anything particular to say about Belgium and the Belgians, foreigners have saddled the nation with the reputation of being dull. It's a hard label to shake off: it is like being asked by someone predisposed to boredom: 'Can't you say anything interesting?' Belgians know this feeling only too well. They've tried.

A curious and endearing characteristic of the Belgians is that they do not rise to the bait that this labelling imposes. Let other nations crow: the cock that crows loudest will be the first for the pot.

But those who scoff should beware. Belgian things are becoming fashionable, and not just the chocolates and the beer. Visitors to Belgium are discovering with shocked surprise the genius of Belgian cuisine, the genuine welcome of Belgian hospitality, the gem-like brilliance of

Flemish art, even the odd château tucked away in the countryside. The group of fashion designers known as The Antwerp Six have risen to international stardom and the fashion department of the Antwerp Academy of Fine Arts continues to produce a stream of head-turning talent. Other nations are beginning to see that, by the standards of 21st-century Europe, the Belgians in their quiet, undemonstrative way seem to have got many things just about right. As if to reinforce this notion, reports published by the United Nations have rated Belgium the best place to live in the European Union, and the fifth most prosperous country in the world (after Norway, Australia, Canada and Sweden), facts which came as a shock to the Belgians who promptly devoted a large quantity of printer's ink to explaining why such accolades are not justified.

Nationhood

The Belgians' lack of fervour for their country may be in part because the Belgian nation is so new. It achieved its nationhood in 1830, after centuries of occupation and invasion by the Romans, the French, the Burgundians, the Spanish, the Austrians, and the Dutch.

Independence was won through a revolution triggered by an opera. Stirred by the sentiments of Auber's *La Muette de Portici* (The Dumb Girl of Portici) the opera-goers rushed into the streets of Brussels in their finery and raised the national flag over the town hall. After a few skirmishes, the occupying Dutch troops fled and the rebels stormed the Royal Palace, where they celebrated the end of Dutch rule by crowning a bust of the King with a Dutch cheese, and wandering through his apartments admiring his wardrobe. These events may lack the heart-stopping panache of the French Revolution, but the

2

Belgians have always opted for moderation at the expense of a place in the history books. And by and large this attitude seems to have served them pretty well.

Belgian-ness is not, therefore, deeply rooted in history. Unlike other similarly new nations, such as Germany and Italy, Belgium is not defined by language either, since it has two main languages: French and Dutch (formerly called Flemish but now referred to as Dutch by Belgians who speak it).

The average Belgian may look modestly prosperous and content, if a little careworn with the stress of so much comfortable domesticity, of the *embarras du choix* of consumer goods, and all the excellent food. But barely concealed beneath the surface of a placid country that might take pride in its lack of national chauvinism lurk strong loyalties to, and bitter antipathies between, the two main language groups.

During the 1990s Belgium was virtually divided into two federal states, Dutch-speaking Flanders and French-speaking Wallonia, stitched together by national government and the capital city – a mainly French-speaking bubble surrounded by Flemish territory.

"*Il n'y a plus de Belges*," is a common complaint. "*Il n'y a que des Wallons et des Flamands.*" ("There aren't any Belgians any more. There are only Walloons and Flemings.") Today nationalism refers to a fervour not for Belgium, but for Flanders or Wallonia. Emotions can run very high and result in unedifying spats between the two communities, especially at the muddy interface along the border. Their respective emblems, the Walloons' cock and the Flemish lion, could well be pictured trying to claw each other's eyes out. At times the very future of Belgium seems in doubt. "We're the only country that wonders if it even exists," claims Belgian poet Daniel De Bruycker. It is often said that there are only two slender threads holding the nation together: the royal family and

3

the 'Red Devils' (the national football team).

As politicians from both communities exploit the antagonisms between the Dutch and French speakers on the principle of 'divide and rule', calling yourself Belgian (as opposed to Flemish or Walloon) has itself become something of a political statement. Car stickers proclaiming *'Belge, et fier de l'être'* ('Belgian, and proud of it') are not some rather desperate bid to shake off a stigma, but an expression of the desire to see Belgian nationhood preserved.

How the Belgians See Themselves

The Belgians are rather too ready to belittle themselves as a nation. They tend to describe their country as being flat and small – in fact, it is neither that small, nor that flat. They seem to expect an insult. Even the towering 19th-century King of the Belgians, Leopold II, scourge of the Congo, once famously dismissed his nation as *'petit pays, petites gens'* (small country, small-minded people).

Despite the many good things that have been said and written about the Belgians in recent years, a certain melancholia and lack of confidence still hang over the nation. They have the best intentions, but something always seems to get in the way: war, economic problems, ill-health, political corruption, the Flemings, the Walloons, the French... or just being Belgian.

When their couturier Dries van Noten first discovered that the international fashion world was almost blindly interpreting 'Made in Belgium' as a label for something really desirable, he was genuinely nonplussed. Belgium is not generally accorded this kind of cachet for high quality, unless you're talking chocolate.

In any case, many Belgians would say that they don't

see themselves as Belgian at all, but as Flemings, or as Walloons, or as Flemings/Walloons first and Belgians second. For instance, in Flanders, a Fleming who becomes an international star is likely to be championed as a great Fleming, but a Walloon who becomes an international star will be claimed by the Flemish as a great Belgian.

What all Belgians share, however – apart from the beer, the chips, Tintin, the Catholic Church, and being roped together by 2,000 years of history – is a sense of not being any other nationality. They may be reluctant to call themselves Belgians, but they are certainly not German, not Dutch and not French. This sets the Belgians apart: few nations are defined by the negative.

How the Flemish See Themselves

The Flemish think of themselves as hardworking, honest and dependable. Look at Bruges, Ghent and Antwerp, a magnificent trio of cities, with their great cathedrals and wonderful collections of art by Jan van Eyck, Dirk Bouts, Rubens, Jacob Jordaens, Van Dyck. These were virtually city-states in their day, and still have an air of individual civic pride and autonomy about them.

Today the Flemish stand proud: they feel that their star is in the ascendant, and after centuries of being kicked around by the French-speaking Belgians they know that the boot is now on the other foot.

The tables have turned. As the old heavy industries of Wallonia collapsed, new light industries and the port facilities in the north, as well as tourism, have brought an economic renaissance for Flanders. It is now ranked as one of the most prosperous regions in Europe, leading the rest in information technology, pharmaceuticals and electrical industries. To the Flemish this is manna from heaven and they do little to conceal their glee. 'Flanders:

Star Region in Europe' ran the slogan of a promotional campaign. It is an overdue counter-offensive to a long history of bad press. The Flemish see themselves at the sharp end of the European economic revival. They pride themselves on their honesty, good nature and humanity, and feel they are cultured in a way that could not be labelled ostentatious. In fact, very Belgian.

How the French-speakers See Themselves

The French-speaking Belgians are more likely than the Flemish to see themselves first and foremost as Belgians. The truth is that they are passing through troubled times. They see themselves as being between a rock and a hard place.

The French-speakers have lost power. They have lost the initiative in a land in which they were once the undisputed masters. Wallonia is taking on the aspect of a pleasant, sleepy province somewhere vaguely in Europe.

The French-speaking Bruxellois see themselves as even more threatened. Encircled by Flanders, they find that the Flemish want to make Brussels the capital of Flanders, despite the fact that the majority of Bruxellois are francophone. ("It depends how you draw the map of Brussels," retort the Flemish.) In a word, the French-speakers of Belgium consider themselves oppressed. They find this hard to accept, for they see themselves as hardworking, dependable, good-natured, sociable and cultured (but not excessively), and rather undeserving of their current predicament.

How the Flemish See the French-speakers

The Flemish cannot help feeling a little smug (if not downright vengeful) about their new-found ascendancy over the French-speaking Belgians. In any case, they think the French-speakers are responsible for their own fate: they are complacent, indecisive and disdainful. The Walloons might call themselves easy-going and liberal-minded, bohemian even, but the Flemish see these traits as a tendency towards laziness, libertarianism and degeneracy. To Flemish eyes, Wallonia looks faintly scruffy and disorganized. Here is a joke which the Flemish tell about their French-speaking compatriots:

Q: Why do the Walloons have a cock as their emblem?

A: Because it's the only animal that still sings while it's standing in shit.

What really annoys the Flemish, though, is the money. The Flemish (unemployment 7%) make profits and pay taxes to the national government, which then promptly redistributes it in welfare payments to Walloons (unemployment 18%). Why should the Flemish subsidize the indolent Walloons? Let them pay for their own sloppy ways.

This is if they can be bothered to think about the Walloons. In Flemish cities such as Bruges you might be forgiven for thinking that there isn't a French-speaking part to Belgium. You rarely hear French spoken. Many of the Flemish believe they could happily live without the Walloons at all.

How the French-speakers See the Flemish

All right, say the French-speaking Belgians, so the tables have turned, but it's just typical of the Flemish that they want to ram the fact down our throats. They won't speak French to us even though they know how; they put up signposts in Dutch – even in predominantly French-speaking areas of Flemish communes; and now they have the effrontery to suggest that Brussels should be the capital of Flanders.

But if this all seems unnecessarily aggressive, petty-minded and vindictive, what can you expect from *les paysans flamands* (Flemish peasants), a humorless, narrow-minded race, with a big chip on its shoulder?

That said, many French-speaking Belgians do, in fact, have close friends and relatives who are Flemish, and who somehow manage to buck the trend. This produces that warm, comforting feeling, particularly after a good lunch, that they are all Belgians after all.

How the Belgians See Others

In contrast to the Byzantine complexities of intercommunal strife within their own country, the Belgians are admirably tolerant of other nations in a most natural, unself-congratulatory fashion, as if this was all part of the good manners and civilized behaviour which they expect of themselves and others.

Considering the Germans have overrun Belgium twice this century without so much as a by-your-leave, the Belgians are remarkably magnanimous towards them. The best that can be said about how the Belgians view the Germans is that they tend to feel emotionally numbed by them. In Belgian eyes, one of the prime reasons for the European Union is to keep the Germans reined in.

The Belgians are a little troubled that they should be more grateful to the Americans than they are. You can hardly blame them, however, for they receive their information about that great nation primarily through the medium of American sitcoms and B-movies (in French areas badly dubbed), a kind of intellectual dry rot.

They view the British as a noble and eccentric nation

which has historic bonds with Belgium that stretch back at least 1000 years. (William the Conqueror was married to the daughter of the Count of Flanders.) They feel the British are making asses of themselves over membership of the European Union and their abstinence from the Euro and are totally baffled by this, but then a nation that drives on the wrong side and whose national game is cricket cannot be expected to behave logically.

Special Relationships

The one thing that Belgians cannot abide, particularly the French-speaking Belgians, is to be asked if they are French. True to life, it sends Agatha Christie's Belgian detective, Hercule Poirot, into near apoplexy.

It has sometimes been suggested that, if Belgium split in two, the Walloons might like to realign themselves with the French. They would rather die, or be condemned to an eternity of British hotel food. The Belgians dislike the French with the kind of inborn passion that most Englishmen would recognize. The pride of the French in their own nation is, to the Belgians, the best argument against nationalism. How could the French, a nation so intelligent, be so laughably misguided? It is not just that the French are haughty and disdainful, they are particularly haughty and disdainful about the Belgians.

What really irks the Belgians is the way the French purloin famous Belgians and are happy to allow the world mistakenly to believe that Jacques Brel, Johnny Hallyday, Tintin, Georges Simenon, et al., are French. The unpalatable truth is, however, that successful Belgians are – or certainly in the past have been – happy enough for the world to make this mistake. Despite all their protestations, many Belgians have good French friends who have somehow miraculously managed to be the exceptions that prove the rule about their compatriots. They are also happy to holiday in France, and would not dream of drinking wine from anywhere else.

The Belgians are not particularly fond of their northern neighbours, the Dutch. To the Walloons, the Dutch are a rather successful, refined version of the Flemish; they are enviably ordered, clear-headed and open-minded, though they lack the secretive and faintly disreputable side of the Flemish with which the Walloons feel more comfortable. To the Flemish, the Dutch are a rather successful European neighbour who happen to speak a language that is similar to their own. However, they are unforgivably mean and puritanical, and drive badly. They stream across Belgium in their caravans during the annual summer exodus, and don't spend any money.

Somewhat oddly, both the Walloons and the Flemish call the Dutch 'the Americans of Europe' because they eat poorly, dress in an unashamedly eccentric way, and are culturally inept when travelling abroad. This insult appeals to a Belgian respect for economy: why offend just one nation when you can offend two?

How Others See Them

The French have always unleashed torrents of withering insults and abuse at the Belgians, and make them the butt of their jokes. Here is a comparatively tame example:

> Two Belgian lorry drivers arrive at a bridge which has a height restriction warning plastered all over it. It reads: Maximum height 4.5m. Their vehicle is 5m high. They stop the lorry and one jumps out and walks into the tunnel under the bridge. Moments later he trots out again, jumps into the cab and says, "OK, let's go! *Il n'y a pas de flics*! [There are no police about!]"

French jokes about the Belgians, however, appear to be going out of fashion. This is not because they are now seen as politically incorrect (not a concept much discussed in France), but because the French are becoming increasingly aware that the Belgians live rather well, have had the good sense to line their nest with all the benefits that playing host to the European Union brings (the sort of self-advancement that the French respect), and have some of the best restaurants in Europe. Renegade French gourmets have even had the nerve to suggest that Belgian cooking is better than their own.

The Dutch attitudes towards the Belgians run parallel to those of the French. They joke about the Flemish being mean (tit for tat) and have a battery of dreadful jokes about them being stupid. Here is one of the better ones:

> Two Flemings are travelling along in a car. Suddenly the driver gets it into his head that one of his indicators is not working. He asks his companion to check it for him. His companion gets out of the car, and the driver switches on the indicator. "Is it working?" he calls.
> "*Nee mijnheer* [no, Sir]," comes the reply. "*Ja mijnheer* [yes, Sir]...*nee mijnheer* ...*ja mijnheer*...*nee mijnheer*... *ja mijnheer*."

How the Belgians Would Like to be Seen

The Belgians would be very happy indeed if all the world knew them to be good-natured, tolerant, individualistic, self-assertive, modest, moderate, and the embodiment of European ideals. This is a long-term project. Meanwhile being placed somewhere on the map of Europe will do.

Character

The Essential Belgian

Four hundred years ago Pieter Bruegel the Elder, the greatest of this great family of painters, captured the spirit of his fellow countrymen busily beavering about their villages, skating eagerly on a frozen pond, or celebrating a country wedding, rosy-cheeked with wine and beer, bursting out of their trousers with all that good food, and falling over their comfortable wives in a jolly rustic dance. The hardware has changed, but the spirit remains largely the same.

The Belgians know how to enjoy themselves, but good fun depends upon sound business. Get out there, do an honest day's work for a fair wage, put some away for the future, then spend what's left over on having a good time. This, essentially, is what Belgian-ness amounts to.

To a Belgian, common sense is a better friend than original thought. Common sense, hard work, humour and tolerance towards outsiders – within reason – are virtues closest to the heart of the Belgians, and the only area of experience where they are suspended is in dealing with each other. When Flemings talk about Walloons and Walloons talk about Flemings, all that virtue and good sense goes flying out of the window.

Burgher Heaven

A pleasure in material comforts, dignity, self-sufficiency and a sense of civic responsibility and good-neighbourliness are the ideals of a good Belgian burgher.

The Belgians like to think of themselves as practical, down-to-earth, dependable. A good Belgian woman knows how to run a household, knows the right temperature for the beer, can cook steak to perfection, shops efficiently at the megastore and holds down a job. Her husband holds down a job, drinks the beer, eats the steak and spends the weekend proudly changing his own oil sump gasket.

Many Belgian families, descendants of the merchants, traders, artisans and guildsmen who shaped this country, exude an air of right-mindedness, self-containment and neatness, which to some outsiders might seem almost stifling. By and large, people conform. If everyone could have a family of two children (a boy and a girl) and a shiny new car, Belgium would be a paradise.

Belgians like above all to be practical, solid. They stand square and conduct conversation from the base of the neck. Courteous behaviour is expected: it is the natural product of right-mindedness. It is also practical: that is how you get on in the world.

They are almost naïvely devoted to being good citizens. Any kind of vandalism, dropping litter, or deliberate anti-social behaviour is greeted with horror and disgust. Social pressure is often sufficient to ensure that, by today's standards, little of this goes on. This is fortunate, because when Belgians fantasize about what society should do with such offenders they conjure up the kind of punishment that shows how close their roots lie to their medieval past.

Enthusiasms

Beneath all that social conformity lurks a nation of strongly moulded individuals – an individuality expressed less in unconventional dress and behaviour than in enthusiasms, some of which can be all-consuming.

Belgians can be passionate about their jobs, whether they be vets, soldiers, sewage workers, cheesemongers. A recent survey showed that 70% of Belgians are happy in their work – 10% more than the British or the Italians.

'I love West Africa,' said the parasitologist from Ghent, thrilled to be back in Senegal. 'For me this is paradise. I love the people, I love the villages. But most of all I love it because it has so many parasites!' More often, however, the job is only a means to fund the real driving passion for some activity pursued out of office hours, at dawn, dusk, weekends and through the night: cycling, football, gardening, dogs, stamps, computers, racing pigeons, etc.

Belgians are avid collectors. A corner of the garage, a cupboard in the bedroom or an entire suburban house is likely to contain evidence of this: definitive collections of matchboxes, early typewriters, tin soldiers. Dotted round the nation are pocket-sized private museums, open to the public, of locks and keys, porcelain figures, tombstones, lace bobbins, old clocks... Brussels alone can claim to have had museums devoted to chicory, birds' nests, lifts, fencing (the sport), even underpants – the elusive private accumulation of an anarchic film maker.

One collection was triggered by a car accident which for a while left taxi-driver Mr. Alfred David with an odd gait. Comments that he 'walked like a penguin' spurred him to turn his home into a museum devoted to penguin paraphernalia – from toys and figurines to beer mats and biscuit wrappers, including a penguin suit in which 'Alfred le Pingouin' wished to be buried. His house became so crammed that his wife apparently presented him with an ultimatum: either all the clutter left or she would. It went, and he with it.

Bizarre collections do not bother the Belgians: they like enthusiasts, as long as it stays within the bounds of decorum, of course. And if they do not have their own private equivalent of a penguin museum stashed away in a shoe box under the bed, they rather wish they did.

Beliefs and Values

Class

The Belgians have a simple class system: everyone is middle class. Belgium is a monument to the values of the middle class, and its values are the ones that they hold most dear.

There are rich and poor, good families and less good families, but the democratic educational system and easy social mobility mean class hierarchies are not a big talking point. It is a great sin, however, to be *vulgaire* (pronounced with a shudder in the voice). This does not mean low class so much as boorish, or lacking in social graces.

Belgium does have a handful of old aristocratic families who own large estates and modestly splendid châteaux. They can still command considerable respect – provided they behave themselves.

The Dream Home

The Englishman's home is his castle. The Belgian's home is a fortified manor house. All around the big cities, greenfield sites are gradually being taken over by pocket-sized gabled and turreted residences, complete with exposed beams, huge open fireplaces, hunting trophies (some crafted in plastic), the odd firearm or semi-antique weapon of war, stained glass in the windows to give the interior the suitable gloom of gravitas, and tiled floors to conjure up Vermeer-like images of the Golden Age of the Low Countries.

These tiles are also highly practical, so easy to clean, to sweep, scrub and polish. Belgians have a horror of dirt and their homes are kept fearsomely clean. You might put rugs over tiles in lip service to comfort, even if your guests regularly helter-skelter across the room on all that polish and do themselves an injury. But wall-to-wall carpeting is looked upon with disgust as an appalling dust trap where scurf and mites and bits of food could lurk undisturbed for days.

Regular household cleaning is carried out as a matter of course, and there is still a tradition among some house-wives known as '*faire son samedi*', whereby Saturday is devoted to a weekly form of spring-cleaning. This even extends to scrubbing the flagstones on the public pave-ment outside the front gate.

As a result, many Belgians end up living in a semi-baronial showhouse in which the heavily over-furnished living room – polished, dusted, and with the abandoned smell of a church vestry – is left unused, and the husband is relegated with his bottle of beer to a room in the basement. The kitchens are immaculate: some so immaculate that their owners prefer to eat out so as not to spoil them.

It is best if your fortified manor house or town flat (which can be treated and furnished in the same vein) is brand new, double-glazed, and fully centrally heated to a temperature just short of a hothouse. This allows you to grow more indoor plants with which to block out the light. A particular favourite is *sansevieria*, otherwise known as mother-in-law's tongue. These do not collect the dirt, require minimum upkeep and deter burglars.

A solid house sitting in its own plot of land, with a double garage attached, is the dream. Some of the garden might be designated as a patch of intense horticulture, but the rest will be laid to lawn, punctuated by a few rather desolate conifers. If this all looks brand new, so much the better: the idea of a mature garden is not widely appreciated. The garden is likely to be primarily the preserve of the family pet, a vociferous and sometimes vicious mongrel that will launch itself at the perimeter fence with sudden, heart-stopping violence as soon as a pedestrian appears before him. It is not clear whether the fence is designed to keep strangers out or the dog in, but it all helps to promote the impression of the inviolable terrain of a *seigneur*.

To achieve this, the Belgian will not have had to abandon his deep roots as artisan and entrepreneur. It is quite likely that the entire set-up will have been built by the hands of the owner himself, from wheelbarrows of cement to the shingles on the turret roofs. The Belgians are incorrigible *bricoleurs* (DIY enthusiasts). The huge and prosperous DIY superstores that have mushroomed on the outskirts of every town do not just sell curtain fittings, wallpaper and paint, but materials for serious structural work. Day in, day out, husbands in lumberjack shirts, sleeves rolled up, walk the aisles in a state of bliss comparing the relative merits of this or that grouting or gutter joint.

An Impressive Lack of Show

The Belgians cannot abide ostentation. *Bon chic, bon genre* (abbreviated to BC-BG), meaning smart and upper-crust, is virtually a term of abuse. When it comes to consumerism, they can be very snobbish about eating in the right restaurants and shopping in the right shops, but they are bitingly critical of snobbery in others. Cutting people down to size is something that the average Belgian can do with surgical precision.

A classic Belgian hero is the cyclist Eddy Merckx, five times winner of the Tour de France. He is now running a successful cycle business, yet he remains without pretension (pretension is a terrible sin in Belgian eyes). All Belgians have an Eddy Merckx story, usually about his understatement. Asked how he had managed to continue a race after remounting following an accident in which he received a double fracture of the jaw, he replied: "Well, conditions weren't ideal, but..."

Grand villas surrounded by shaded parks, sleek cars, shopping at the international couturiers, frequent holidays in exotic places, annual winter sports – such things are *signes extérieurs de richesse* coveted by the Belgians, and exploited ruthlessly by advertisers and glossy magazines. In fact, very few people partake in such lifestyles and, when it comes down to it, few would want to. It's all too snobbish, too remote from real life: where are the jolly family gatherings? Where are the chips with mayonnaise?

Success is measured in more modest terms: the best thing is to earn a good living and stash away enough money in various pension schemes and numbered Luxembourg investment accounts to retire at a youngish age, then to live long and comfortably and to pursue hobbies, grow vegetables and enjoy plenty of extended lunches in good restaurants with pals who share the same outlook on life.

Religion

Eighty per cent of Belgians are Roman Catholic. What this means, in effect, is that every community has its church, where the locals get baptised (and sugared almonds are dished out in porcelain figurines of swans and cherubs), confirmed (looking like angels at an age sensibly too young to argue), married (the opportunity for an immense beanfeast), and formally despatched to the afterworld (the entire community, friends and enemies and complete strangers, will attend).

Besides these rites of passage, the average Belgian will

not bother the Church unduly. People use birth control, they divorce, unmarried couples live together. Priests keep a low profile, drink, smoke and play bridge with their parishioners. They are not the ubiquitous reminders of the ever-present threat of sin as they are, for instance, in Ireland. One cannot help thinking that the Belgians started to leave God out of their social circle some time during the last world war, but feel that it would be a waste to let all those nice buildings become redundant. Most households still have a few crucifixes pinned to the wall, for instance in the spare bedroom – just in case.

Resident Foreigners

The word 'foreigner' has a specific meaning in Belgium. It refers to 'the immigrants' – not the thousands of European, Japanese and American businessmen and government officials who live and work in Belgium, but the North Africans (*Maghrébins*, i.e. from the Maghreb) and the Turks. Here their good-natured tolerance of outsiders often crumbles.

The immigrants came as guest-workers to do the dirty jobs which Europeans disdained. Now they have large and well-established communities in many of the cities. In some of the central districts of Brussels 50% of the population is of immigrant descent. There is little social contact between most Belgians and these immigrants, except when the former go for a cheap couscous in a North African restaurant. Most of the immigrants do not drink alcohol so, for them, that writes off about 80% of Belgian social life. When things are going well, the Belgians ignore the immigrants; when things are going badly, the Belgians see them as 'a problem'. They accuse them of sponging off the state, of dishonesty, crime, begging, and, worst of all, ingratitude.

Behaviour

Rulers of the Roost

Belgian men like to think they rule the home. It is run according to their rules, with their money, in their time. Their wishes are paramount. Belgian women find there are just about enough rewards in married life to justify allowing their husbands this fantasy, and only rarely draw attention to the fact that it is actually they who do most of the cooking, shopping, budgeting, social organization and raising the children, not to mention the thinking. The most efficient matriarchies are cleverly disguised as patriarchies.

In later life this ascendancy is no longer disguised. The Belgian matriarch reigns supreme. In place of a helmet and visor is a weekly perm of stiff, fawn-tinted curls and large plastic-rimmed glasses; in place of armour a gaberdine raincoat belted firmly around the growing midriff; and in place of the trident a handbag filled with discount vouchers from the supermarket chains. She will sweep gracefully about the neighbourhood in the company of other like-minded matriarchs, shopping and lunching, and join coach parties to Paris and Santiago de Compostela. Her husband, now well-trained and with little ambition, will be left at home to feed the dog, clip the hedge, take messages and reminisce over a few beers with chums from his youth who have been similarly abandoned – and are touchingly grateful for it.

The Family

The family holds strong ties in Belgium. Many weekends feature visits to other members of the family, if only for a ritual peck on the cheek and a snatch of gossip before flying off to the shops. Instead of doing anything to avoid them, adolescent children will often voluntarily seek out the company of aunts, uncles and grandparents, and can expect a handout as a reward for humouring them. Eating with the family and relatives is a major pastime.

Most people have family living close by. Indeed, in a country where major cities such as Brussels and Antwerp are separated by just 35 minutes on the motorway, it is hard to live far away. Once upon a time every family had a granny in the attic. The modern Belgian household, however, is strictly nuclear, but granny is often just a block away, conveniently placed to field the children when they come home from school, and to dispense her wisdom about how to keep your man.

Weddings, in particular, offer excuses for major family get-togethers, and Belgians take great pride in proving to themselves just how widely they can spread the net. After the formalities, guests settle down to some serious eating and drinking, and often round off the evening with a dance. The idea of the British wedding at which children are not welcome because they might disrupt the proceedings is greeted with complete disbelief: marriage is surely a celebration of family life, and ultimately about having children, isn't it? How can they be excluded?

Until recently, it might have been said that the ideal family in Belgium consisted of a Fleming married to a Walloon bringing the children up bilingually. There are many such families in Belgium. Sadly, however, their status has been undermined by the political polarization of the two communities. It is no longer such a virtue to marry someone from 'the other side', and integration has become harder for the spouse living away from his or her own community. This has led to a sense of bewilderment. It is like the honest dairy farmer suddenly finding the world is full of militant vegetarians.

Children

Belgian families used to be enormous. This was officially condoned, and indeed there is still a tradition by which the seventh consecutive son becomes automatically the godchild of the King and is baptised with the King's name. At the funeral of King Baudouin in 1993 a church was set aside to accommodate this rather specialized form of royal godchildren, and the service was relayed on screen from the cathedral in Brussels. There were no fewer than 600 seventh sons, all called Baudouin/Boudewijn. The seventh consecutive daughter likewise becomes the Queen's godchild, but the incidence of this is, apparently, much more rare.

The majority of Belgian children are balanced, sensible, constructive, and polite, and younger ones – fresh-faced, natural and neatly turned out – are often absolute winners. In fact, Belgian children are generally so well behaved that British parents tend to think there must be something wrong with them. Even adolescents become bad tempered in a rather endearingly old-fashioned way.

If a youth misbehaves, has his headphones on too loud in the metro, or drops litter, he or she is liable to be berated by another member of the public, probably a busybody pensioner brandishing a walking stick. Offending children found guilty in court of vandalism will face the ultimate sanction – their parents will be fined. Wait until they get home.

Elders

Belgium shares with Germany the honour of having the highest percentage of over-55s of all the countries in Europe. They can count themselves lucky, because by and large they are well treated. From birth Belgians are taught to respect, obey and finally take care of their elders, and even the most crotchety, meddling and divisive old grand-parent will be tolerated and humoured, albeit with much gnashing of teeth. Generally, however, the elderly are rather artful in their strategy of advancing age: as a quid pro quo they tend to be supportive and tolerant of their children's mistakes, and try their best to be good company. It all comes back to Belgian practicality: we all have to get old.

But you can have too much of a good thing. When the elderly can no longer look after themselves, they tend to move into old people's homes and sheltered accommodation rather than join the family. In the main, these are sympathetically run, allowing as much independence and family access as a resident wants or can bear.

Sex

The Belgians are practical about sex, but not prudish. *'On garde un homme par son ventre et son bas-ventre'* is a characteristic piece of Belgian wisdom ('You keep your man by [catering for] his stomach and what lies below it'). Georges Simenon claimed to have slept with 10,000 women, so clearly there was something amiss in his household. His wife – perhaps in defence of her cooking – contested his total: she put the figure at 1,200.

Driving

Gone are the days when the best advice on seeing the red-and-white Belgian numberplate was to pull over on to the hard shoulder and start deep-breathing. The Belgians now have driving licences. In fact, they've had them since the early 1960s. Before that, drivers had been able simply to get in a car and go.

Many older Belgians learnt to drive during the war

when someone pointed to a lorry and threw them the keys. When eventually licences were introduced, anyone over 18 could claim one – you couldn't after all expect experienced drivers to go through the humiliation of passing a test. For years this test consisted of nothing more than a written examination of the tick-the-box variety about the rules of the road. Driving an actual car for real did not come into it.

Unlike the Italians or the French, Belgians do not see driving as an extension of their sex life. However, they do pride themselves on the speed of their reflexes: this can be the only explanation for piling down the motorway at 90 miles per hour two yards behind the vehicle in front. The concept of 'stopping distance' is not much aired. Over several generations this virtue will be firmly established in Belgian genes, since those without the necessary reflexes will not survive long enough to reproduce.

Belgian cars are the objects of love, a statement of one's position in the world and by and large technically pretty much state-of-the-art. All cars have to undergo a severe, if somewhat arbitrary, mechanical test at regular intervals. Unlike the eminently corruptible British MOT system of testing by privately owned garages, in Belgium the tests are run by government agencies, and they take no prisoners. If your lights don't work, or your exhaust emits unacceptable levels of pollution, it's back to the garage until you can pass muster.

That said, Belgians have not entirely abandoned the view that driving is a form of Russian roulette, an opportunity to gaze upon mortality. They drive around the 'Ring' which encircles Brussels as if they want to fill the void left by Jackie Ickx's retirement from Formula I racing. This includes lorry drivers.

Furthermore, they doggedly cling to *priorité à droite* (called *priorité de droite* in Belgium) as if it were some kind of inalienable human right. It is true that roads are increasingly being marked with 'give way' signs, but on an unmarked road you are perfectly at liberty to launch into a junction without so much as glancing left to see if anything is coming. As a result, it is a mistake to relax on any country road, and it is disastrous to do so in a city.

Belgians will tell you that giving way to the right is madness, ridiculous, lethal. But do they still insist upon it? Certainly. It's a right. It would be tantamount to cowardice not to. Besides, what else could deliver that delicious frisson in an otherwise mundane world?

Manners and Etiquette

Greetings

It is important to acknowledge people fully on every meeting in Belgium, with a triple kiss to relatives and friends (even fairly new and casual ones), or by shaking hands with more distant friends and acquaintances, and with a hello to shopkeepers, petrol station attendants, waiters, etc. Failure to do so may draw the conclusion that you are unforgivably rude or up to no good. Since everyone knows everyone else in a Belgian village (and everything about them), a Belgian progressing through his or her own patch will dance a kind of pavane of kissing, handshaking and waving.

Boys expect to be kissed by both women and men up to adolescence, but close male relatives and old chums will also plant firm kisses on each other's grizzled cheeks until the grave. Saying please, thank you and goodbye with appropriate elaboration is a habit inculcated from infancy, and the reluctant child will be dragged kicking and screaming across the floor to elderly relatives to deliver the obligatory thank-you kisses.

Gifts

The Belgians are quite embarrassingly generous with gifts. When they come to stay, or just come to dinner, they are liable to bring chocolates (top-quality, Belgian chocolates), wine, flowers and a gift for the children. Birthdays are never missed, and Christmas is a time of spectacular generosity when no-one will be left out.

Flowers are presented on the flimsiest pretext. Florists are respected members of society and every community will have several, selling an astonishing range of very fresh blooms.

If you do not reciprocate in kind – it might be ruinous to do so – the Belgians are not in the slightest bit put out. The pleasure of giving is genuine, and once done is forgotten. There is no hidden profit and loss account. However, persistent failure to show willing at least will be noticed eventually and count against you. The Dutch, apparently, have done this as a nation. One of the Belgians' major criticisms of the Dutch is that they do not give gifts.

Queuing and Gossiping

In shops and in chance encounters in the streets, gossip is exchanged with rapid-fire efficiency – who is in hospital and what for; wasn't it a good funeral; whose husband has been inexplicably delayed in Namur, again. It is amazing how much news can be exchanged in the time it takes a *charcutier* to slice an Ardennes ham or a *boulangère* to wrap a *baguette*.

Everyone must wait their turn. It is obscene to push in, and two customers in a line may exasperate a pressed shopkeeper by shuffling backwards and gesticulating endlessly to insist that the other goes first. Politeness and deference are so much a part of Belgian life that the rare outbreaks of rudeness appear as an outrageous affront and leave the victim quite breathless. Unless, of course, you are a Walloon in Flanders, or a Fleming in Wallonia, where you can only expect to have your worst prejudices confirmed, and might be disappointed not to.

Food and Drink

Live to Eat

If there is something that the Dutch and the French-speaking Belgians have in common, it is a delight in food. The food of Belgium is now acknowledged as among the very best in Europe, and many of its restaurants have earned all kinds of the most respected international garlands and awards.

The cuisine is essentially French, and though many of the top-rated restaurants are in Flanders, even the Flemish accept that the language of *haute cuisine* is French. Whereas in the last two decades French cuisine in France has fallen victim to fussiness, over-elaboration of visual effect, and quasi-scientific dietary dogma, Belgian chefs have kept their feet firmly on the ground. The Belgians wouldn't have it any other way: they like good cooking which respects the innate qualities of first-class ingredients. They treat pretentious cooking with the same scorn as overpriced cooking: they vote with their feet. Restaurants that are not up to scratch quite simply fail. Competition is so great (there are over 3,000 restaurants in Brussels alone) that restaurants which do not give the customers what they want cannot survive.

Good, honest food, prepared with craftsmanship, is what the Belgians like. These standards apply equally to the *charcutier*, to the *pâtissier*, even to the owner of a humble chip-van, as much as to the great and grand restaurants. Belgians also like to be well fed. There is an old tale of Victor Hugo in a Brussels restaurant. 'I can see, sir, from the amount of bread you eat,' said an inquisitive fellow-diner, 'that you must be French.' 'I can see, sir, by the amount that you eat,' retorted Hugo, 'that you must be Belgian.'

The Belgians do indeed like to eat plentifully, and take their time about it. Children regularly accompany their parents to restaurants, and are helped to endure the two or so hours that lunch might take not only by being given whatever they want from the menu (Belgians become gastronomes from a tender age), but also by arriving armed with toys, magazines and colouring books to keep them occupied.

Lunch often drifts into late-afternoon coffee, when sumptuous tarts will be set out on the table back home and forced into any remaining vacant corners of the digestive tract. These are the crowning glory of the *pâtissier*'s art, exquisitely made pastry filled with custard, cream, fresh fruits and fruit-jelly or chocolate. Every community has its expert *pâtissier*. Indeed it might be considered the ultimate in social deprivation if it did not.

Office workers eat well. Numerous restaurants special-ize in providing a limited selection of excellent value-for-money lunch dishes, served on the trot. Due attention must always be given to food.

Belgians think nothing of driving for a couple of hours to the coast for seafood or to a restaurant celebrated for its *paling in 't groen* – eels in green sauce (made from spinach and mixed herbs such as sorrel, watercress, chervil, mint, parsley, lemon thyme and sage).

All this interest in food does have its downside, however. Because Belgians expect great things from their food and their standards are extremely high, disappointment can be profound. Every popular restaurant has at least one glum table where stout elderly diners eat silently, without joy, muttering criticisms about how such-and-such a sauce was better when so-and-so was the chef, when the world was a better place, before their health fell foul of all that food, all that drink and all those chocolates.

Chocolates

The Belgians are famous the world over for their luxury chocolates, or pralines, as they are called. Foreign chocolate makers often buy their raw materials from Belgium. Dark chocolate is made from the best cocoa beans and contains a high proportion of cocoa butter and cocoa solids (usually over 52%); 'white chocolate', made mainly of milk and cocoa butter, is a Belgian speciality; and only the Belgians seem to have mastered the technique of producing chocolates with fresh cream fillings on an industrial scale.

They also sell them on an industrial scale. The chocolates are comparatively cheap, so a Belgian is as likely to buy a kilo of Leonidas chocolates as a bunch of flowers. The specialist outlets are permanently busy: white-gloved assistants either fill up boxes with the customer's own selection of favourites from the trays behind the glass counter, or dish out ready-packed boxes for the client in a hurry. High consumption produces high turnover produces low prices: the perfect formula for successful Belgian business. Every citizen helps the GNP along by dutifully consuming an average of 7.8 kilos of chocolates each year.

Chips

Belgian chips are the best in Europe. Cut to the size of a lady's little finger, they are fried twice to make them perfectly crisp, served with a dollop of mayonnaise, and often eaten behind the curtain of rain dripping from the awning of roadside chip-vans while the traffic thunders by.

Drink

Drinking is a major leisure activity, but few Belgians see drink as the means to get drunk. Indeed drunkenness is an affront to social decorum: the odd lapse will be forgiven, but the offender will be mercilessly ribbed about it for years to come.

Some Belgian commuters still pop into a bar near their train station for a little tipple to help them on the way to work. This practice has declined in more health-conscious times, but the 'bar without a key' (i.e. open 24 hours a day) is still alive and well, frequented by a broad cast of characters, from the burly lorry drivers delivering seafood to restaurants in the early hours to the trim office staff putting the seal on another day's work. There are also the gravel-voiced habitués who are permanently propped up against the bar, where they may even take a nap.

The really distinctive characters are the female bartenders – spry, breezy women of uncertain age, dressed in black skirt and white apron, who can maintain four acrobatic conversations at once, take an order from a table of twelve without writing it down, and pitch any unwelcome client into the street by the ear. Even male bar staff seem to hold them in awe, and tend to hover behind the beer taps shining glasses with a cloth.

Drinking is mostly focused around food. However, it may begin about two hours before eating and continue until two hours after it. Apéritifs are popular. These may include a glass of port, or one the restaurant's 'house apéritifs' (often a fearsome brew of startlingly lurid colour), or some thick medicinal liquid made of extract of artichoke and orange (thought to be good for stimulating the appetite). Belgians also drink wine – French wine – in prodigious quantities, but the undisputed national drink is beer.

Beer is Best

A hundred years ago there were over 3,000 breweries in Belgium but many of these have been subsumed by larger breweries with the result that today there are a mere 110. These still manage to produce nearly 1.5 billion litres of beer per annum under 600 different brand names and labels (of which 37% is exported). Drinking an average of almost 100 litres of beer a year, the Belgians rank sixth in the world (just behind the Czechs, Irish, Germans, Austrians and Danes).

Stella Artois, produced by the giant conglomerate Interbrew, is the best-known brand, but it is the Trappist beers (e.g. Orval, Chimay, Westmalle) which make the connoisseurs watery-eyed. These are still brewed under the strict control of Cistercian monasteries, although nowadays mainly by lay workers. Sold in bottles, they are readily available in supermarkets, but in the interests of quality the monks resolutely resist pressure to increase production to feed a huge potential export market.

There are many other beers of distinction, including the wheat beers often taken with a slice of lemon – a tasty pick-me-up for mid-afternoon. The valley of the River Senne has its own unique, naturally occurring airborne yeast which is used to produce a distinctive, winey beer called *lambic* and its derivatives: *kriek* (macerated with cherries), *framboise* (raspberries) and *faro* (caramel and sugar). The famous *gueuze* is a matured form of *lambic*.

Most bottled Belgian beer has three vital statistics on the label: the strength of the beer, which ranges from a stronger-than-lager 5% to a stratospheric 12%; the temperature at which it should be served; and the type of glass into which it should be poured. Each brand of beer has its own preferred style of glass, from an elegant tapering vase shape to a stemmed chalice. Every bartender knows instinctively which beer goes in which glass; a slip-up could be considered a sacrilege that will render the beer virtually undrinkable.

Health

Say 'How are you?' to a Belgian at your peril.

The Belgians are very concerned about health – their own health and anybody else's. It is a major topic of conversation, and once engaged upon, is liable to evince all the grisly details of symptoms, emissions, what the pharmacist said, what the doctor said, what the specialist said, and what Mrs. Maertens next door said about her husband who had the same thing, before he died.

The health of a nation is closely related to its diet, but this is not the kind of theory liable to make you friends in Belgium. The fact is that all that drink and excellent, rich food tells. Digestive problems, constipation, gout, indigestion, all are common concerns, commonly aired, and greeted with great sympathy. Homespun wisdom will usually advise drinking only one colour of wine, avoiding *pâté de foie gras* for the time being, or drinking a herb tea after any major meal. But yes, do have another drink and another chocolate, if that is what you feel like: happiness is the best medicine. If things get worse, the average Belgian has a medicine cabinet crammed full of pills left over from a catalogue of past illness or kept in readiness for any that may lurk over the horizon.

Pharmacies and Hospitals

When home cures do not work, a Belgian will go first to a pharmacy. These are awesomely efficient enterprises, smelling of costly perfumed cleanliness, where highly trained staff in starched white coats tap the keyboards of on-line computers and dispense wisdom from their impressive battery of knowledge. They have such advanced medical knowledge that it is often not necessary to go to a doctor at all, although they are very precise about the limits of their jurisdiction.

Pharmacies are part of a general health system, part-private, mainly government funded, of which the Belgians might be justly proud. Many of the hospitals are modern, with up-to-the-minute equipment, staffed by doctors, nurses, ancillary workers and administrators who are well trained, capable and inspired by a genuine dedication. The Belgians' great concern about health ensures that anyone working in this field is accorded respect, admiration and great appreciation.

Leisure and Pleasure

Holidays

Belgians jet off all around the world on package tours and self-constructed adventures, just like any other brand of European. But true Belgian holidays are spent on home ground – in the forests of the Ardennes or among the dunes of the bracing North Sea coast. Camping, caravanning, cycling, fishing, watersports are all part of the fun. The inevitable drizzle will add to the sense of achievement and family unity.

The outdoor life engenders healthy appetites. From the

neat, tree-lined avenues of the campsites, from beneath the awnings of tents, from garden-shed-like cabins lining some bosky river, and from the mighty residential caravans whose wheels have not turned for decades, emanate the sounds of laughter, of cutlery on plates, the uncorking of bottles, and the rich aromas of sizzling steaks, grilled fresh fish, melting chocolate, and sauces to die for.

Holidays are essentially a time for family fun, but may also be the cause of family strife. Many Belgians (especially men) keep their nose so close to the grindstone, year in, year out, that an innocent enquiry such as "Going on holiday this year?" can precipitate a hideous change of mood in a family gathering. Some fathers have to be dragged away from their desks for a holiday, and leave claw marks all the way to the homestead. The tensions leading up to the holiday may induce symptoms of sickness that only go away when the day for the return to work dawns.

Sometimes it is clearly better for families to avoid the issue of holidays altogether and to pack the children off to organized summer camps in the Ardennes or at the sea. Here, in a safely cocooned, scout-like atmosphere, children learn campcraft, play volleyball, and go canoeing, and explore the intense adolescent experiences which their parents try to steer them clear of for the rest of the year.

La Mer/De Zee

The Belgian sea coast must be one of the most unprepossessing in Europe. Bitter winds funnel in across the North Sea, looping over the ranks of mighty dunes and sand-blasting the unsightly apartment blocks and amusement arcades. The string of resorts is interspersed by wind-battered caravan parks, connected by dreary roads and bypasses, crisscrossed by railway lines and canalized inlets from the sea.

Yet for many Belgians there is a great romance about La Mer. It is the scene of famous holidays spent paddling in the grey sea, strolling along the promenade eating *gaufres* (waffles) powdered with icing-sugar and cornets of freshly fried chips, sheltering in the warm pockets of sunlight behind the beach-huts and windbreaks, riding on the crazy bicycles and other beach-side attractions in a state of exhilaration. And then there is the seafood – from the winkles sold from a van, along with the pin, to the cornucopias of fresh shellfish, lobster and crab piled high on platters and placed in the centre of a table of glowing faces.

The Belgian sea coast may not be exotic, but it is not pretentious either. It is a place of old, reassuring certainties: the predictably dire weather, occasionally interrupted by long, scintillating, ozone-filled summer days; the worn apartments rented by the same families year on year, where the infants of one generation later return with their own. The Belgian sea coast is, in effect, quintessentially Belgian. The only foreigners here are those who appreciate it for that very reason.

Sport

Some Belgians are passionate about sport, particularly football. Devoted fans will spend every evening in the supporters' club bar, surrounded by trophies, scarves, photos of great players and championship tables, discussing the last game or the next. Some even play the game.

Meanwhile cyclists whizz around the countryside in dangerous gangs called *pelotons*, clad in buttock-hugging shorts and the latest Tour de France strips.

Many of them turn out to be aged over 60.

Belgium has its own home-grown heroes in Grand Prix motor racing, rallying, cycling and judo, and has produced a clutch of international tennis stars – somewhat to its own surprise. Foremost among them are Kim Clijsters and Justine Henin, who have both reached the position of No. 1 in the world's women's tennis rankings. In soccer, Anderlecht and the Bruges team Club Brugge stand among Europe's best. However, the racy nickname of the national football team, the 'Red Devils', seems only to tempt fate.

The trouble is, sport is not considered vital to life in the same way as good food. In all the brouhaha of a major championship victory, Justine Henin commented that it was 'only tennis'. Obsessive drive and killer instinct – essentials to modern sporting success – are not really part of the Belgian psyche. Eddy Merckx was the exception. His appetite for victory earned him the nickname 'The Cannibal'.

Shopping

There is a French expression '*faire du lèche-vitrines*': literally, 'licking shop windows'. It means window-shopping, but its image of salivating consumers is not too wide of the mark in Belgium. Belgians love to shop, a passion amply catered for by the shopkeepers who overwhelm the senses with the pure visual abundance and intrinsic elegance of their wares, be they clothes, furniture, toys, cheeses, sausages or light fittings.

The Belgians are sticklers for quality. If they do not like a cut of meat, they will tell the butcher, and if they should ever get something that is past its sell-by date (Heaven forbid), they will publicly tear a strip off him. All communities have their collection of high-street shops and each of these is usually a specialist: the florist, the *pâtissier*, the butcher, the hardware store, the pharmacy, the stationer. What they sell is quite clearly defined – shopkeepers do not tread on each other's patch. Each works hard to earn the loyalty of their customers, pampering them with gift wraps, elegant printed carrier bags and showers of polite and interested, and at times transparently ingratiating, conversation. Shopping is a pleasure, but the hard-headed client always makes it quite clear, in the politest way, that he or she has a choice.

One of those choices is to go to the local megastore, or one of the glamorous new malls, all plate glass, polished brass and marble, that are springing up in the cities and bigger towns. The Belgians love a bargain, and will shop for basics in these supermarkets, but they miss the specialist skills, human contact and the pampering of their own local shopkeepers. And so it is that, against the odds, local high streets have survived.

Humour

The Belgians like a good laugh. Professional comedians tend to play on puns and quick-fire repartee: "Tongue? Yuck! The idea of eating something that has been in a cow's mouth disgusts me." "Do you eat eggs then?"

The commonly peddled set-piece jokes are often somewhat leaden, and are usually met with a patient smile and a polite chuckle. What really gets Belgians laughing around the table in a bar or restaurant is the real-life tale of some incident that happened at work, in the train, in the supermarket, at the hospital – stories of confusion, mistaken identity, tales of the antics of well-known 'characters'. Here is an example:

One day in a commuter train, where everyone knows just about everyone else, and people chatter or play cards, a prim, elderly lady took out her handkerchief to blow her nose. She waved the handkerchief to unfold it, but it slipped from her clasp and floated to rest on the lap of an old man slumbering on the seat opposite. Unfortunately, as everyone was aware, his flies were undone. Fellow passengers spotted the elderly lady's predicament, and watched eagerly to see her next move. She hesitated, then leant forward to retrieve her handkerchief. As she did so, the old man woke up, and saw all faces turned towards him. Looking about him in sleep-befuddled panic, he realized that his flies were undone. Hastily he pulled the zip up, stuffing the handkerchief into the opening as it closed. The elderly lady was caught in mid-movement...

It would be unfair to say that the Belgians cannot laugh at themselves, but they do not make a habit of telling jokes about themselves either. Why make yourself the butt of a good joke when you can tell it about the Flemish/Walloons instead?

Culture

Belgium has a rich cultural heritage but the nation has simply not been around long enough to acquire the cultural roots to which the label 'Belgian' can be attached and made readily identifiable. The Belgians themselves are not greatly perturbed by this. Just as they are perfectly happy to watch American films on their Japanese televisions, drive French cars, and read romantic novels translated from English, they do not attempt to place Belgian culture on a larger stage than it deserves.

Decorative Arts

But it's always a mistake to underestimate this nation. Every now and then, from the manicured ranks of city terraced houses, from the sleepy comforts of suburbia or solid rural villages, a conventional cocoon will burst open and out will flutter a magnificent butterfly, throwing the conformity of Belgian life into stark and dramatic relief in a flourish of inspiration, experimentation and inventiveness. This is the nation which produced the Surrealist painters, René Magritte and Paul Delvaux. Of the two, Paul Delvaux was perhaps the more overtly Belgian – all those dreamy nudes reclining in moonlit tram stations.

The Belgians were at the forefront of the avant-garde in the late 19th century, hosting exhibitions by Cézanne while his own nation reviled him as a crackpot. The Symbolists emerged during this period, producing a highly varied array of mystical, emotionally charged paintings – artists such as Jean Delville, Léon Frédéric, Fernand Khnopff and Léon Spilliaert, who converted Belgian gloom into inspirational stylishness. Some two decades before the advent of Expressionism, the Anglo-Belgian James Ensor was painting bizarre, frenetic oils with titles such as 'Skeletons Arguing over a Pickled Herring'.

This tradition of being at the cutting edge of controversial modern art has been revived in recent times, notably through the dynamic public galleries of Ghent and Antwerp. Hot artists include Wim Delvoye, whose notorious *Cloaca* installation (first shown to acclaim in New York) eats, digests and excretes food twice daily.

It was a Belgian who brought the revolutionary nature of Art Nouveau to architecture. Victor Horta designed the world's first Art Nouveau house in Brussels in 1893. His studio and house (now a museum) demonstrate his unparalleled genius for beautifully stated, flowing design.

Art Nouveau was all the rage throughout Belgium until the First World War, and involved a number of key designers such as Henry van de Velde, who founded the Kunstschule in Weimar, which became the Bauhaus. Sadly, much of Belgium's Art Nouveau heritage was destroyed when it went out of fashion, but a great deal still remains, spawning a new category of Belgian enthusiast – the Art Nouveau spotter.

Scratch a Belgian and you will find a Surrealist – although he or she may deny it vehemently. Public monuments underpin a penchant for incongruous imagery. The Belgians, and more particularly the Bruxellois, have virtually adopted as emblems the Atomium (an outlandish, giant model of an iron atom, 100m tall, erected for the Exposition Universelle de Bruxelles in 1958), and the Manneken-Pis (the little bronze fountain of a naked boy urinating, which is regularly dressed up in one of his 650 beautifully made costumes donated by regiments, societies and foreign governments, each specially tailored to allow him to continue to function as a fountain).

The Belgians do not really trumpet about culture at all. They like the idea of it, but distrust anyone who displays too much. They are not at all keen on prima donnas. The actor/author Noël Godin and his team of 'entarteurs' (pie throwers) have made a speciality of ambushing any public figure they consider to be too self important – artists, film makers, industrialists, politicians – with cream cakes (Bill Gates was a famous victim).

Even Magritte, one of the few artists to have become a legend in his lifetime, insisted upon his ordinariness to the point of eccentricity: like an office clerk, he would breakfast, put on his hat and coat, hang his umbrella over his arm, kiss his wife goodbye, then walk round the block, re-enter the house, hang up his brolly, hat and coat, put on an overall and begin his day's work at an easel in the corner of his dining room.

Cops and Comics

The great figures of Belgian literature include Maurice Maeterlinck, Emile Verhaeren, Michel de Ghelderode and Hugo Claus whose most famous work is entitled, revealingly, *The Sorrow of Belgium*. All are virtually unknown outside the Low Countries and France. Talk of popular literature, however, and you have two figures of world class. Simenon, the pipe-smoking writer of some 300 novels, is one of them. 76 of his books featured Inspector Maigret. His work has been translated into 87 languages, making him one of the all-time most-read authors in the world.

The other one is Hergé, the influential practitioner of the comic strip, or *bande dessinée*. (His real name was Georges Remi: he simply took his initials GR and reversed them). He is best known for Tintin, the roving boy-reporter, who carried with him on his travels many of the characteristics and ideals of the Belgian nation.

Bandes dessinées are a serious pursuit in Belgium. At the Centre Belge de la Bande Dessinée (the Comic Strip Museum) in Brussels, transfixed adults pore over rank upon rank of archive comic strips. Not a laugh nor a giggle intrudes upon the awed solemnity of this shrine.

Television

Most Belgian households receive about 30 channels via cable from France, the Netherlands, Germany, Britain and Luxembourg, and many will tend to watch any of these rather than home-produced Belgian fare, for which there is no great enthusiasm.

The state-owned television and radio companies are naturally divided in two: the French-speaking and the Dutch/Flemish-speaking. And never the twain shall meet. Both sides' news broadcasts, current affairs programmes and documentaries maintain an impressively high standard, but their entertainment programmes consist mainly of a dehumanizing fare of quiz-shows, American movies and ancient television series, and crude Feydeau-like farces in which all characters will at some point hide in a cupboard in their underwear.

Television advertisements are generally modest, often somewhat amateur, and with fewer of the big screen mega-productions with which the British attempt to sell a car, buried within a mini-plot from *Fatal Attraction*. The Belgians want to know about the car, not whether it offers an increased opportunity for extra-marital affairs. Advertisements are interspersed with the stations' jingles, which are about as subtle and as mind-piercing as a mechanical road digger.

Despite everything, the Belgians watch an awful lot of television. But if torn between that and an opportunity to eat, drink and socialize, television does not offer much competition.

Nightlife

Eating and drinking are the main form of evening entertainment in Belgium, which makes it a little hard for any alternative enterprise to get off the ground. But Brussels has a raft of funky dance clubs (garage, house, 'tchak-boom-tchak'), while Antwerp has acquired a reputation for its lively club scene which is so mercurial that if the details of any club appear in a listings magazine, it is probably already out of fashion.

Trendy bars are similarly subject to the merciless whims of fashion. One week the 'in' bar will be packed to the gunwhales, and the tunes of the decorative ragtime pianist will be drowned by the din; the next week you will be able to hear every note he plays. Expressionism, post-modernism, 1950s retro, minimalism – every style has been bent to the bar-owners' need to trap a crowd. On Fridays and Saturdays such places can reach a pitch of feverish excitement.

At quite the other end of the spectrum are the old *cafés-dansants*, where elderly, silver-suited bandsmen strum out syrupy Belgian hits of yore to the widows and their flamenco-suited gigolos on the dance floor – lowlife scenes straight out of the songs of Jacques Brel.

To most Belgians this great singer-songwriter is the only Belgian musician who really matters. Drawing from traditions of the ballad and the music hall, Brel conjured up songs of great power and range – funny, cruelly satirical, poetic, deeply romantic – that had universal appeal and at the same time captured the very essence of Belgium. People talk with misty eyes of the Brel concerts they attended in their youth and, on hearing *Amsterdam* or *Ne Me Quitte Pas* broadcast yet again across the airwaves, will be stopped in their tracks.

Le Plat Pays (*This Flat Land*), an evocation of Belgium in the weather brought by the four winds, is a classic portrait of the nation. Here is the third verse:

> With a sky so low that a canal becomes lost in it,
> With a sky so low that it engenders humility,
> With a sky so grey that it will hang itself for it,
> With a sky so grey it has to be forgiven for it,
> With the North Wind that comes and blows itself apart,
> With the North Wind, listen to it crackle,
> This flat country of mine.

Custom and Tradition

Carnivals and Fairs

Should you have any doubts that surrealism has historic roots in the nation's psyche, you only have to attend one of the traditional annual carnivals or processions. Giant papier-mâché figures of medieval folk characters are paraded through the streets of small market towns amid raucous brass bands and copious beer-swilling. The participants relish a day of time-honoured revelling, but the civic pride, the official stamp of approval, and the weight of tradition generally conspire the drain such events of the vital oxygen of spontaneity leaving the spectators' faces frozen into bemused grins.

Like many other fun-loving Catholic countries, Belgium runs a particularly strong line in pre-Lenten carnivals. In the most famous, held on Shrove Tuesday at Binche in western Belgium, male participants called Gilles parade in elaborate traditional costumes resembling upmarket court jesters, with bells, lace collars and cuffs, and bizarre pink masks, complete with wire-rim spectacles and moustaches, tied on with a kind of bandage. Later in the day they put on towering headdresses of white ostrich feathers and throw oranges at onlookers. No-one seems to know quite why.

In May, at the *Kattefeest* of Ypres, cats made of cloth are hurled from the tower of the town hall; these days they are made of cloth, but up to 1817 they were the real thing. In August, a deracinated may tree is paraded noisily around the streets of central Brussels by the Brotherhood of the Companions of St. Lawrence, and then replanted in a pavement. So the list goes on.

Most Belgians can take or leave such set pieces. But where their faces light up is at the funfair. Annual funfairs take place throughout Belgium, but the most famous is the *Foire du Midi* which occupies half of a major thoroughfare of western Brussels in July/August. There are shooting galleries, dodgems, helter-skelters and the latest state-of-the-art lunch-revisited rides which reduce the good burghers to quivering, shrieking, exhilarated wrecks. This is also the official kick-off for the shellfish season, so those not partaking of the rides settle down at trestle tables to demolish plates of mussels, whelks and winkles and down glasses of cool beer. For a Belgian, that's real fun.

Religious Festivals

Despite the nation's apparent indifference to religion, ancient veins of Catholic fervour are tapped for religious festivals – sometimes to an unsettling degree. At the *Boet Processie* (Procession of the Penitents) in Veurne in the northwest, people march solemnly in spooky, hooded monks' outfits carrying crosses. In Bruges a phial of Holy Blood is paraded around the streets on Ascension Day, amid processions of people dressed in medieval and biblical costume. Any suggestion that the Bruggelingen (the people of Bruges) are simply putting on a show to inflate yet further their flourishing tourist trade can be quashed by the fact that they have been doing this for 800 years.

Easter is a quiet affair, valued mainly as a public holiday and celebrated on behalf of children who hunt Easter eggs which the *cloches de Rome* (bells of Rome) have somehow magically managed to hide in the garden.

Belgian children have two Christmases. The first is the *Fête de Saint-Nicholas* on 6th December, when they are showered with presents and may visit St. Nicholas in his grotto at a shopping centre. Dressed in his costume as the Bishop of Myra, he is accompanied by *Zwarte Piet*, his blacked-up, whip-bearing assistant. Then at Christmas proper, the family get together on Christmas Eve for an elaborate evening meal, after which they go rolling off to midnight Mass and a good singsong. On Christmas Day the children are showered again with gifts, but these are often of the more sensible kind, such as clothes.

Another important date in the social calendar is All Saints' Day on 1st November. In the gathering gloom of the approaching winter, the cemeteries become filled with astonishing quantities of flowers, in particular chrysanthemums, glowing with their autumnal colours. The following day is the *Jour des Morts*, when virtually everyone pays respect to the family dead, and which many interpret as not so much a Christian rite as a remnant of the Belgians' Celtic past.

Systems

Law and the Police

On a day-to-day level, the Belgian police are generally thought to be doing their best, but if you were a Belgian, you would probably think that the best is not good enough. The recent tide of revelations about corruption and incompetence simply confirms a deep-rooted mistrust in the commitment and motives of all authorities. 'Shock, Horror!' scream the headlines, to which the Belgians roll their eyes and shrug their shoulders, reflecting an equally deep-rooted sense of powerlessness.

In truth, these problems are probably the product of a system that dates back to medieval times, to the days when armourers, cordwainers, herring-salters, tallow-chandlers and barber-surgeons called the shots. As they go about their business today, running petrol stations, growing begonias, baking pastries, bottling pharmaceuticals, propagating Internet companies, the Belgians perpetuate a rather opaque moral code. On the one hand they appear honest and law-abiding to an almost painful degree. This leaves them dangerously exposed to utter dismay whenever crime – from burglary to car-jacking by pistol-toting gangs (something of a local speciality) – bursts in upon their neatly ordered communities. On the other hand, they believe in a system of mutual favours – "it's good for business" – which leads to a corrosive atmosphere of petty, or not so petty, corruption.

Such contradictions were brought centre-stage by a series of extreme incidents that have erupted over the last couple of decades, which include random killings in an orchestrated series of unsolved supermarket raids, grisly murders, political assassination, large-scale government corruption, and colossal food-safety scandals.

These high-profile events transformed the national mood. Belgium, formerly rather sweetly provincial and naïve, was suddenly confronted with a different, sinister vision of the modern world. There was much eye-rolling and shoulder-shrugging, but this time the Belgians were truly shaken. Many took these events almost personally; they felt a sense of national humiliation which reawakened the age-old underlying lack of self-esteem. Every Belgian citizen seems to have a theory about each of the cases – usually involving conspiracy. But at the heart of the problem lies the penetration of civilian life, including the justice system, by political influence and cronyism.

The Belgians have done much to come to terms with these traumas and have emerged rather like the faithful purged by confession. They would dearly like to draw a line under them, but their antiquated and inadequate legal system prevents them from doing so. Although arrested in 1996 for his part in a shocking case of child abduction, paedophilia and murder, Marc Dutroux, the nation's most reviled prisoner, was only finally convicted in 2004. His case became mired in an unending catalogue of scandal and deplorable incompetence, and hung over the Belgian nation like a guilty conscience. And what really riles the Belgians is the suspicion that all the while he has been luxuriating in some cushy jail at the tax-payers expense, surrounded by the sort of material comforts that most downtrodden Belgians dream of.

Politicians are promising radical reforms but Belgians – reinforced by a new-found cynicism – are not holding their breath.

Education

According to a United Nations report, the Belgian education system is the 'best in the world'. This is just the sort of good news that the government seizes upon in relieved triumph, and which is guaranteed to elicit a grumpy dismissal from any teenager actually going through it.

Belgian schools are divided into three main categories: the state-funded local schools, open to all comers; more disciplinarian, single sex, Catholic schools which are fee-paying but heavily subsidized by the state; and expensive private and boarding schools which cater only for a tiny minority of children, often those with special needs. The vast majority of children, from the plumber's daughters to the industrialist's sons, go to the local, free, co-educational school, where they can expect a solid education, good enough to give them the qualifications needed for higher education if they so desire.

A high level of discipline is expected, and if any child steps too far out of line and is repeatedly disruptive, the school will take sanctions, and talk to the parents. If this doesn't have any effect, other parents will talk to the parents. That usually works.

Children walk or bicycle to school, or take the bus,

neatly dressed in clean, everyday clothes. On their backs they carry satchels, usually the subject of fierce competition: at the *rentrée* (start) of each academic year, only the most fashionable satchels will do, usually inscribed with slogans and names from the latest cult television shows or movies. Most children would not be seen dead with last year's satchel.

Universities, like the schools, are separated by Belgium's linguistic divide, and few students cross over. This issue was dramatically brought to a head at Leuven/Louvain, one of Europe's oldest universities, where Flemish was treated as a secondary language until violent discord in the 1960s caused the university to split. As a result, the French-speaking community earned itself a spanking new university town called Louvain-la-Neuve ('New Leuven'), south of Brussels, for which they are rather grateful.

Roads and Railways

Belgium has the only major motorway system in the world which, except for the new section stretching out towards Dunkirk, is lit at night in its entirety. Apparently this can even be seen from space.

Belgian trains are staffed by railworkers with the kind of motivation expected only in bobsleigh teams. They turn out in neatly pressed uniforms and wield their ticket punches with gestures moulded on the parade ground. While they inspect your ticket they will show off their encyclopædic knowledge of Belgian railway timetables by telling you, in two languages, where to change trains, when your connection departs and from which platform, and when it arrives. One suspects they all live in converted signal boxes and have been running model trains since infancy. It makes for a system of enviable efficiency.

Government

The Monarchy

In 1831 the Belgians scoured Europe for someone to take up the post of King of their new nation. After a few rejections, the offer was eventually accepted by Prince Leopold of Saxe-Coburg-Gotha, an uncle of Queen Victoria. Being a Protestant, he was not considered perfect, but he took to the task and married a daughter of the King of France, thereby engendering a Catholic dynasty.

Thereafter, Belgian kings married a string of foreigners, so there is barely a centilitre of Belgian blood in them at all. It seems to have served them well. Although maintaining a low profile, they play an important constitutional role as head of state, and the royal family is widely admired and respected. The fact that they have married wisely, and stayed married, has helped.

The King is a symbol of Belgian unity. This was made graphically clear at the death in 1993 of King Baudouin, a shy, modest and dignified man, when over 125,000 people waited in the rain outside the royal palace in Brussels to file past his coffin and pay their last respects.

Compared with most other European monarchies, the Belgian royal family remains relatively untroubled by scandal, and its place in the affections of the Belgian nation has been reinforced by the next generation. Baudouin was succeeded by Albert whose son and heir Prince Philippe married Mathilde d'Udekem d'Acoz, a Belgian aristocrat with roots in both Flemish and French communities. Her natural charm has melted many hearts and strengthened the royal family's stock by holding out the prospect of becoming the first truly Belgian Queen.

The ancient Salic law (which excluded male inheritance) was abandoned in 1991, so Philippe's eldest child, a daughter (Elisabeth), is second in line to the throne after her father and ahead of her younger brother – practical evidence of the Belgian monarchy's willingness to adapt to modern ways, which may prove the key to its long-term survival. Meanwhile the Belgians have become fixated with the Princess who is pictured on stamps and in magazines dressed in pretty cotton frocks redolent of the 1950s, indicating that a strong dose of nostalgia – for a rose-tinted vision of the elegance and innocence of times past – also underpins the popularity of the Belgian royal family.

Divide and Rule

'The Belgian Compromise' describes essentially the way in which Belgium was created out of two separate, linguistically divided communities to make a single harmonious whole. The Belgians' capacity to find a solution through compromise in any sphere is sometimes also referred to in the same vein. However, in the context of nationhood, the term has rather lost its shine.

The issue of federalization (the process by which government is being devolved to the increasingly autonomous federal regions Wallonia, Flanders and Brussels) remains the great political football, exploited to some degree or other by politicians of all colours. The Flemish are the most vociferous 'nationalists'. An extreme right-wing party called the Vlaams Belang ('Flemish Interest') lays claim to the Flemish nationalist cause. Formerly named the Vlaams Blok, in 2004 a court judged it to be racist and forced it to disband. The re-grouped VB still commands over 20% of the vote in Flanders and has consistently strong support in Antwerp, which gives the large immigrant and Jewish population the jitters. The Walloons cannot cry foul: they also have correspondingly extremist parties (albeit commanding a much smaller percentage of the vote).

The national government of Belgium generally consists of a rickety coalition of Socialists, Liberals and Christian Democrats, precariously patched together with minority religious and sectarian parties from both sides of the sectarian divide. When Guy Verhofstadt – a 47-year-old Dutch-speaking Liberal – became prime minister in 2000, he headed a coalition of six parties, no less. Belgian politicians are raised on compromise.

Given this state of affairs, the Belgian government can sometimes produce some startlingly controversial legislation. Belgium was the second country in the world (in 2001, after the Netherlands) to introduce legal euthanasia (assisted death) for incurables in a condition of 'constant and unbearable' suffering. It also has legalised gay marriage. However, its daring legislation (passed in 1993) to permit the prosecution of any crimes against humanity, no matter where committed, turned out to be a law too far. When too many world leaders began to fall under its spotlight, the practicalities of diplomatic fudge prevailed, and in 2003 the law was replaced by another with a far more modest and parochial reach.

Ministers of the national government do not have a great deal more power than their counterparts in the regional governments of Flanders and Wallonia, although certain areas such as defence, taxation and infrastructure, still remain in the domain of national, as opposed to regional, government. Democracy is enforced by law: all eligible citizens must vote, or face a fine.

The King has to give his assent to any legislation passed by the national government. This gave rise to a famous incident in 1990, when King Baudouin was confronted with a bill to make limited abortion legal. He objected on moral grounds, but to avert a constitutional crisis he abdicated for one day so the bill could be passed. Widely admired as a sensible solution to a moral impasse, it was also clearly a classic case of Belgian compromise.

Business

Belgium seems like the quintessential home of the small businessman: tiny family enterprises still run decorating firms, shops, garages, cleaning services. Men in their grey *cache-poussières* (work coats) open their electrical repair shops at the crack of dawn in eager anticipation of another day's business, and women shopkeepers will busily scrub the floor and threshold of their shops at the end of the day before locking the door and depositing the takings in a night-safe.

These days, however, business in Belgium is dominated by large conglomerates, many of them foreign or multinational such as SUEZ (energy, water, environmental services), and the old pharmaceutical and chemical giant Solvay. Nonetheless, the impression on the ground remains quite different.

There is little sentimentality about Belgian business. From the individual shopper and restaurant-goer upwards, commercial instincts are sharp, and unforgiving: the market rules. Take the market for souvenirs, for instance, about which Belgians show no shame. You can buy Manneken-Pis corkscrews, Tintin keyrings, quasi-medieval instruments of torture, and underwear with the Atomium printed on it. Even lace has been dragged into the tourist trade.

Lace was once the province of the ladies of the numerous *béguinage*s – semi-religious settlements (and refuges) for single women awaiting an offer of marriage, or death. As fashions waxed and waned, so did the demand for lace. The 19th century was lace-crazy, and there were some 50,000 lacemakers in Belgium. These days, machine-made lace from the Far East has made barbaric incursions into the painstaking traditions of handmade lace. Proper Belgian lace is still made by hand, and is available – but at a price that will always limit its appeal to lace aficionados.

Antwerp is famed for its hard-nosed approach to business. At some distance from its old medieval heart is has the second-largest port in Europe (after Rotterdam) with 80 miles of docks. At night the surrounding refineries transmogrify into a magical world of a trillion star-like lights set against the eerie orange glow and deep roar of giant flares. Antwerp is also the world's diamond capital. This staggeringly profitable business, handling 85% of the world's uncut diamonds, is crammed into an unglamorous square mile near the railway station where diamond jewellery is sold by the shovel-load to those who prefer to think that that bargains are forever.

Brussels, Capital of Europe

To some Europeans the very name Brussels is like a red rag to a bull. They see it as the source of the evil of Euro-centralism and unwarranted meddling. Even to the more well-disposed, the European Union is thought of as a bit of an Aunt Sally. Jokes like this are legion:

Q: How many people work in the European Commission?
A: About a third of them.

However, Belgians by and large are strongly in favour of a united Europe. The elegant blue, star-spangled Euro-emblem can be seen on flags, car-stickers, postcards, umbrellas, satchels, note-pads and toothbrushes. Even the Manneken-Pis has his own bespangled Euro-outfit.

The reasons for their enthusiasm are not hard to see. For one thing Brussels is profiting enormously from being the focus of all that attention, and all those funds. In fact, nearly a third of the city's population is made up of foreigners of which over half are European Union nationals.

The EU itself accounts for some 80,000 jobs in Brussels and the number is rising. The financial benefits to Belgium are estimated to be about 4.5 billion Euros (over £3 billion) per annum.

The Belgians want European unity first and foremost because they have seen too many wars fought over their homeland as a result of nationalistic squabbling. Being a trading people at heart, they also want to profit from an open market. Furthermore, if their country is disintegrating into federalism, at least it can do so under the broader umbrella of Europe, where national borders are in any case more fluid, and regions are at liberty to associate with whomever they choose. Indeed, Belgium's lack of a strong national identity probably makes it the perfect nation in which to locate the headquarters of the European Union.

The Suits

To someone not versed in the gulf that separates Flemings and Walloons, it might seem that all Belgian business persons are the same. They wear unflamboyant, shiny suits, carry thin despatch cases and hold forthright business meetings in which jokes and idle chat about golf and gardening are definitely not part of the agenda.

"But we object; we are not at all alike!" declare the Flemish business person and the French-speaking business person in unison. (Most of the business people are, in fact, businessmen.)

The French-speaking businessman, according to the Flemish, is hardly worth taking seriously. He will string a visiting sales force along, showing interest, but refuse to make a decision. The process can take years. Flemish businessmen see the product, make a decision and send their own proposed contract by return of post. This is almost too quick, but hang it if it is a mistake: they'll make up the loss on a concurrent deal.

The Flemish businessman is at his desk at 7 a.m. The Walloon (as his Flemish counterpart sees it) probably leaves the house at 7 a.m., has a croissant and a coffee in a bar, visits his mistress and pitches up at 10.30 issuing terse instructions to his secretary. The Flemish businessman thinks about how he can do more work to earn more money. The Walloon thinks about how he can do less work to earn more money. Essentially, the Flemish see the Walloons as lazy.

According to the French-speaking businessman, the Flemish approach to business is "Me first, and the rest will follow". The Flemish businessman lacks finesse. Business structures in Flanders may be more democratic and open, the bosses may be more technically competent, having trained up through the ranks, but the Flemish will discuss a problem to death to find a compromise. Where's the panache, the imagination in that? The answer is in the bank balance, comes the reply. Flanders flourishes while Wallonia wallows. Here is a Flemish joke about the Walloons' attitude to work:

> A Walloon politician is addressing an audience of workers: "With our economic plan, you can all look forward to enjoying a four-day working week!"
> Enthusiastic applause.
> "And soon after that we'll be offering you a three-day working week!"
> More enthusiastic applause.
> "And then later you'll be able to live comfortably by working just two days a week!"
> Wildly enthusiastic applause and cheers.
> "Yes, and finally you'll have a one-day working week!"
> At this point a voice is heard from the back of the hall.
> "That's great, but please don't make it Monday!"

Language

To get a job in almost any Belgian national institution you need to be bilingual. This puts the French-speakers at a distinct disadvantage as they are by tradition deeply reluctant to learn Dutch. What, they argue, is the point of learning a language that only 6 million people speak? (22 million, if you include the actual Dutch).

The Flemish find it incredible that the French-speakers have so consistently refused to learn their language. It is not unusual for francophones married to Flemings and living in Flanders to be quite unable to speak anything but the most rudimentary Dutch. In revenge, Flemish Dutch-speakers – even those holding government posts in which bilingualism is an essential qualification – pointedly refuse to speak French. With hindsight, one might suggest that the Belgian government should long ago have taken decisive action in the educational system to ensure that all Belgians were fully bilingual. Oh no, say the Flemish with a grin: for if that had happened, the French-speakers would not have so conveniently disqualified themselves from virtually all government posts.

Dutch (formerly known as Flemish)

It's official: the language of Flanders has been rebranded as Dutch, and calling it Flemish is now discouraged. Nonetheless, many people still refer casually to *Vlaams* (Flemish) as a language – though this was never so much a language as a disparate collection of dialects, so disparate that the people of West Flanders find it hard to understand those in the east. At school the Flemish learn Dutch, i.e. *Nederlands*, which is effectively the lingua franca of the Dutch-speaking world, and this enables them to talk to all fellow Flemings, as well as the Dutch themselves (who also have their own dialects).

A minor but significant difference between Flemish Dutch-speakers and the actual Dutch is that, out of political distaste, the Flemish will not use imported French words, such as *coiffeur* (hairdresser), as the Dutch will. The Flemish use either a Dutch word or, if really stuck, an English one.

Walloon

The word Walloon comes from the name of a Romanized Celtic tribe, the Wala, who lived in southern Belgium and developed their own kind of French, which, after all, is a mixture of Celtic and Latin. Walloon is thus a dialect form of French, or rather a collection of regional dialects. Today few people speak wholly in Walloon and the language has all but vanished, preserved in a few words that pepper the language of the French-speakers of Wallonia. For instance, some say *les canadas* for potatoes.

French-speaking Belgians otherwise speak standard French – except that they say *septante* for seventy and *nonante* for ninety – and traditionally have a throaty accent which the French love to mimic.

Bruxellois

Brussels is the third major administrative region of Belgium, neither a part of Flanders nor of Wallonia, although the vast majority of its people speak French. The old language of Brussels was Flemish, but when Belgium was a part of the Duchy of Burgundy, French became the language of the ruling classes and filtered downwards. The locals developed their own kind of hybrid dialect called *bruxellois*, which is mainly Flemish, with bits of French and Spanish thrown in.

There are still a few true Bruxellois who will slide easily from Flemish to French and back again without noticing, spicing their language with earthy words and phrases found only in Bruxellois. For example, a man with wandering hand trouble is a *'froucheleir'*, and a dishonest rat may be called a *'schieve lavabo'* – a crooked basin.

A Sign of the Times

Belgium might be a nation of two languages (plus German, of course), but it is not a dual-language nation. Bilingual labels on products and posters give an entirely misleading impression.

It is quite impossible to guess which language group a Belgian comes from by the surname alone. A De Staercke, Kickx or Verbeeck might well be a francophone; and (although less likely) a Belpaire, Cantré or Le Bon might well be Flemish.

Notices in one language at the linguistic frontiers tend to get daubed with insults in the other language. The names of many of the cities have two forms, and these are given in their local form on signposts. So, if you are trying to steer a path to the French-speaking city of Mons, you have to know that in Flemish you are not going to Mons, you are going to Bergen; nor is it Liège, but Luik; and Namur is Namen. Conversely, the Flemish city of Mechelen is Malines in French; Ieper is Ypres; Veurne is Furnes. Outside Brussels the two communities, polarized by the childish squabble about language, cannot find the good grace to erect signs in both.

The Author

Like many of his generation, as a youth Antony Mason had almost no contact with Belgium, apart from hitch-hiking through it on the way to somewhere else. On one trip he and his travelling companion were picked up by a friendly Belgian driver who invited them home for a meal, a generous act but also alarming since he drove at top speed and insisted on turning round to address long pieces of conversation to the back seat. This reinforced certain prejudices about Belgian driving, which, along with other prejudices about the Belgians, the author has been monitoring closely ever since and, one by one, shedding.

This task has been greatly assisted by fate. In 1975, on the French island of Martinique, he met a beautiful Walloon. He didn't really know what that was at the time, and it didn't seem to matter. She later became his wife. They now live in London with their Anglo-Belgian son, but make frequent visits to Belgium – to Wallonia, Brussels and Flanders – with ever-increasing pleasure.

Antony Mason is the author of some 50 books on travel, exploration, history, antiques, architecture, house plants, espionage, volleyball... In 1995 Cadogan Books published his *Cadogan City Guide to Brussels, with Bruges, Ghent and Antwerp*, the product of three years' work which tested the forbearance of his Belgian family to just short of destruction. He feared that the present book would prove to be the last straw. But like true Belgians, they have displayed admirable tolerance, and total bemusement with the whole enterprise.

Further titles in the Xenophobe's® Guide series:
www.xenophobes.com